TESTIMONIALS

"Kathlyn brings to her work an honesty and a compassion for self and others on the journey that inspires the reader to engage in the process of transformation with the same honesty and self-compassion. In doing the work of this book, I was able to discern that I had allowed memories of past traumas to impede my willingness to be vulnerable enough to set the goals that really matter to me. I would recommend this book to anyone who is ready, or who wants to be ready, to take action on their conviction or to engage in transformation."
– Jennifer Leavenworth, Licensed Marriage and Family Therapist.

"Great, comprehensive guide to get into action and make real positive change. Teaches you how to get out of your own way and take back control of your own life instead of letting life control you. Quick read, great advice and easy to implement."
- Gayle McMahon, MBA, homemaker, mother of two adult children, competitive tri-athlete, married 25 years

"I am not much of a sit-down book reader, however I dove right in. I cannot tell you how happy I am now that I decided to read The Rule of Nines. There are many aspects of the book that caught my attention, the most being how Kathlyn incorporated her very own life experiences, including many of her own hurts, losses, physical/mental frustrations and pains as well. This gave the book credibility. It was also a very informative, but comprehensive read.

"Until now, I hadn't read a book from cover to cover in a very long time. I highly recommend The Rule of Nines. Not only is it interesting, informative and humorous at times, the lessons learned here could, in fact, change your life."

– Todd Reinhold, Retired LAPD SWAT officer, father of two adult children (Divorced x 2)

"This was so good! I finished this book and felt like the message was clear: you can control your mind and thought patterns to be positive by simply choosing to make a step forward, training your mind and actions. Changing your life by redirecting yourself on a more positive path, changing the way you see things! Choosing positive instead of negative."

- Katherine Medina, registered Dental Assistant, licensed Real Estate Agent, Mother of three adult children, Divorced

THE RULE OF NINES

THE RULE OF NINES

A Step-By-Step Guide to Permanent Behavioral Change

LIVE LESS OUT OF HABIT
AND MORE OUT OF INTENTION

KATHLYN HEIM

NEW YORK

LONDON • NASHVILLE • MELBOURNE • VANCOUVER

The Rule of Nines

A Step-By-Step Guide to Permanent Behavioral Change
- Live Less Out of Habit and More Out of Intention

Published in New York, New York, by Morgan James Publishing. Morgan James is a trademark of Morgan James, LLC. www.MorganJamesPublishing.com

ISBN 9781642795462 paperback
ISBN 9781642795479 eBook
Library of Congress Control Number: 2019938260

Cover Design by:
Chris Mendoza
CMD5150@gmail.com

Interior Design by:
Christopher Kirk
www.GFSstudio.com

Disclaimer: The Publisher and the Author make no representations or warranties with respect to the accuracy or completeness of the contents of this work and specially disclaim all warranties, including without limitation warranties of fitness for a particular purpose. No warranty may be created or extended by sales or promotional materials. The advice and strategies contained herein may not be suitable for every situation. This work is sold with the understanding that the Publisher is not engaged in rendering legal, accounting, or other professional services. If professional assistance is required, the services of a competent professional person should be sought. Neither the Publisher nor the Author shall be liable for damages arising herefrom. The fact that an organization or website is referred to in this work as a citation and/or a potential source of further information does not mean that the Author or the Publisher endorses the information the organization or website may provide or recommendations it may make. Further, readers should be aware that Internet websites listed in this work might have changed or disappeared between when this work was written and when it is read.

Morgan James is a proud partner of Habitat for Humanity Peninsula and Greater Williamsburg. Partners in building since 2006.

Get involved today! Visit
MorganJamesPublishing.com/giving-back

DEDICATION

Dedicated to my children, Sean and Kayla, and to the patients I work with and the nurses who serve them. A special thank you to JR for believing in me, and to Connie Pheiff, founder and CEO of the Pheiff Group, and my manager from Talent Concierge, for assisting me in making my dream a reality. I hope the advice you find in this book may prove useful to you no matter where you go in life.

TABLE OF CONTENTS

AUTHOR'S NOTE

After my 17-year marriage failed, I found myself empty, depressed, anxious, and unable to recognize myself. I no longer knew who I was, what I wanted or didn't want, what made me happy, what made me sad, or where I was going in life. It was at this point in my life that I embarked on a personal journey of self-discovery.

That personal journey began with the implementation of daily meditation, journaling, positive affirmations, and expressions of gratitude. I began to read as many self-help books as I could get my hands on. I even sought assistance through therapy and spiritual advisors, only to learn that focusing on the past drove me deeper into the rabbit hole of depression.

I thought, "Why am I focusing on the past?"

I came to the realization that I could not change what already occurred, but I did possess the power to change what came next! I began to look within as well as looking out. I became hyper observant, aware not only of my own thoughts and behaviors, but those of the people around me. I began to study their behavior, as well as my own.

My role as a health educator afforded me the opportunity to work with and observe people of all ages, backgrounds, genders, and ethnicities. Every one of them required and desired to make behavioral and lifestyle changes in order to improve their health, eliminate addictions, and live longer, happier lives. Working with these patients afforded me the opportunity to identify barriers and obstacles to change. I became aware that many of them had become stuck by falling into a subconscious pattern of thinking which led them to acting in ways that sabotaged their own efforts to make progress.

I began to both use and to teach the principles of Motivational Interviewing (MI) in an effort to evoke behavioral changes and improve the health outcomes for others. Although these techniques were very effective in evoking change, there was still a missing piece of the puzzle. The missing piece was the "what." The "what" that came from a mind-body-soul connection that so many of us are lacking.

This book attempts to provide that missing piece of the puzzle by helping to re-establish the mind-body-soul connection. It is this connection that separates The Rule of Nines from all of the other self-help books designed to create behavioral change. As you will learn with further reading, the principles outlined in The Rule of Nines are applicable to absolutely anyone and everyone, regardless of age, gender, sexual orientation, ethnicity, or religion.

If you are ready to create positive change in your life, identify and achieve your goals, overcome your addictions, or erase unwanted behaviors, keep reading. The best is yet to come.

FOREWORD

Unfortunately, life throws us lemons. We may struggle with adapting, face fierce challenges, receive ineffective training, lack support, or be swallowed by comparing ourselves with others. As life gets more complicated, self-empowerment will too.

The self-help genre isn't brand new. In fact, the marketplace is saturated by self-help books. Authors like David D. Burns, (Feeling Good: The New Mood Therapy), Malcolm Gladwell, (Outliers: The Story of Success), Stephen R. Covey, (The 7 Habits of Highly Effective People: Powerful Lessons in Personal Change), Carol Dweck, (Mindset; The New Psychology of Success) and others have all pursued their personal path to happiness by offering advice based on their research and experiences that encourages people to commit to personal development and take back their personal power so they can overcome being greedy, slothful, vengeful, overweight, or addicted.

So why read this book? What makes it different from all the rest?

Heim's step-by-step guide reminds us all that sometimes our greatest achievements and successes come from our greatest challenges. *The Rule of Nines* provides hope. I, too, can honestly say that Heim's teachings have inspired me with the essential elements necessary to achieve personal success. More importantly, Heim gives us the strength to carry on regardless of whether or not others share in our passion.

In today's global landscape, we truly need to remind ourselves that we can overcome and embrace our purpose. It is our responsibility to never let go of our quest, no matter how hard the challenge. Every one of us holds a gift that we are meant to share with the world.

There will always be struggles, setbacks, and heartaches. It's those who pick themselves up by the bootstraps in spite of fear who become our greatest leaders.

Nothing will ever be just right. Nothing will ever be perfect. There will always be obstacles and less than perfect conditions. That's okay. That's life. If you wait for perfection you will never let go. Heim's tools provide you the strategies to pull up your bootstraps and get started today. You will become stronger and more skilled. Most of all, you will find your courage and the confidence to live your life to the fullest.

Within these pages you will discover your special gift. When you do, keep going and never quit. You will achieve permanent behavioral change.

~Connie Pheiff
Founder & CEO, Pheiff Group, Inc

INTRODUCTION

The Rule of Nines was written to help those struggling to make the changes in their lives they know they need to make and to make sure those changes stick. It provides clear action steps to take and will help you understand why you've been failing in the past, even though you've been trying so hard. The Rule of Nines will provide tools to assist in regaining control over your choices and your life so you can finally make progress toward getting the life you desire.

Where You Are

Right now, you're feeling frustrated because nothing you're trying is helping. You feel like a failure as you watch other people succeed, but you just can't seem to get there no matter how hard you try. You desperately want to change, but you're struggling to make change happen. You don't know what it is you are doing wrong.

People are telling you it's because you lack willpower. They tell you it's because you're weak or just don't want it badly enough. But you know that's not true. You know how hard you struggle every day to improve, even though you seem to take two steps forward and three steps back. Despite all the setbacks and failures, you have still not given up.

Where You Want To Be

You want to finally lose that weight. You want to receive that promotion, earn an advanced degree, obtain financial freedom, improve your relationships, put down the cigarettes, lose the drugs or set down that bottle for good. You want to feel the sense of achievement that only comes when you've finally made your dream a reality.

You want everyone who told you that you'd never make it to see how wrong they were. You want every person who didn't believe in you to see that you are not a loser or a failure. You are a conqueror. You are a person who knows what you want and then makes it happen.

Most of all, you want the confidence that comes from having achieved your goals. You want to feel empowered to be your best self and to grow into the person you've always wanted to be.

How This Book Will Help

You are probably asking yourself, "What exactly is the Rule of Nines?" The Rule of Nines (RONs) are rules to help you act with intention in order to achieve success in reaching all of your life goals through behavioral change. This method is simple and individualized.

The first three rules help identify the goal. The next three rules help specify what areas to focus on in order to achieve the goal. The last three rules break the goal down into three separate points. Three rules x three specifics x three points = nine rules or "The Rule of Nines." It is my recommendation that you read this book more than once to fully absorb the content.

Why I Wrote It

Where did the RONs come from? Believe it or not, the RONs came to me in a dream. My life vision has always been to "make a difference," to help people live a better life, whatever that may look like to them. I just wasn't sure how to make that happen.

Should I go on a medical mission trip to a third world country? Volunteer at the homeless shelter? Donate time and money to specific causes? When I woke up from that dream, I no longer had to wonder…I knew. I received a clear picture in my dream: The Rule of Nines. Not only did I know how to help others, I was now able to help myself.

At the time I am writing this, I am 53 years young. I have struggled with my weight since the age of 5, when someone in kindergarten told me I was fat. From that point forward, I struggled with my body image. I began to diet at the age of eight. My parents, pediatrician, and all the children that teased me, decided my goal for me.

Not only each New Year's Day did I "vow" to lose weight, I vowed this each Monday, the first day of each month, each time the wind blew, and each time it didn't. I believe you are "getting it," am I right? Some of you may be laughing. Others may have a tear or two they are holding back.

Needless to say, I still have not lost "the weight." Why? Why have I not lost the weight? Did I hear someone say that I don't have willpower? I will tell you that I have more "willpower" than almost anyone I know. Not only have I not lost those extra 10 pounds, the extra 10 pounds grew from 10, to 20, to 30. Again, why??

Why have I been unsuccessful in achieving my weight loss goal? Well, I am going to tell you. Because contrary to popular belief, my own included, weight loss was not and is not *my* goal.

Losing weight was a goal that society's norms and values told me to have. I was to lose weight to look like what other people thought I should look like. Health did not matter. My soul did not matter. My happiness did not matter.

My lifelong journey chasing someone else's goal for me did not come without a heavy price tag. I have struggled with an eating disorder that has varied from long-term starvation, to compulsive exercise, to consumption of laxatives and diuretics.

Prior to discovering the RONs, I felt like a failure. This took an emotional toll on my self-esteem, my relationships, and most important, my soul. When I discovered that MY goals should be the only goals I set out to achieve, I became successful in the achievement of each and every goal I set for myself.

By The End of This Book

After reading the RONs, you will have gained the ability to differentiate between your goals and other people's goals so you can avoid the emotional havoc caused when we are not in alignment with our soul. It is this misalignment that leads to addictions, affairs, divorce, depression, and suicide.

You will learn how to shrug off the expectations placed upon you for what you have been taught to believe based on society's norms and values. You may feel like time is running out or that you are too old to make these changes, but the good news is, it's never too late to achieve self-awareness. It is never too late to evoke change. It is never too late to lead a happier, more fulfilling life! That journey begins today.

九

Section I:

THE FIRST THREE RULES

Rule 1.

IDENTIFY YOUR "WHAT"

What exactly is a "what?" A "what" is your goal. It is "what" you desire to accomplish. It is YOUR idea for YOUR future. It is the desired result that YOU envision for yourself. A "what" is a specific goal created in order to achieve a desired outcome. A "what" requires a vision, a plan, and a commitment.

Why We Fail To Reach Our Goals

Although it may seem easy to define a personal goal, often this is not the case. As I mentioned in the introduction, I began struggling with my weight at the age of 5 when someone in kindergarten told me I was fat. From that point forward, I struggled with my body image.

At the age of eight, I was told I needed to lose weight. For years, I tried, and failed. No matter how hard I tried, I could not lose the weight. I read every book, attempted every fad diet, and engaged in every exercise program imaginable from belly dancing to weight lifting. In fact, I exercised to the point where I sustained a major injury requiring surgical intervention.

This injury resulted in permanent nerve damage and partially paralyzed nerves in my right leg. This life-changing injury forced me to "slow my roll." My physical life, including work, came to a complete halt.

There I was, lying motionless in my hospital bed, unable to feel much from the waist down, unable to move an inch to either side without assistance. I was newly divorced with two teenage children and had just purchased a home six days prior to my injury. My career as a registered nurse in the emergency department was physical. My life went like this: workout, work, kids, repeat! My mind was racing, "What now?"

I had nothing but time to think about my life and where it was headed. The "down time," or "think time," forced me off that hamster wheel of life that so many of us get stuck on. Running in circles, endlessly, doing the same thing over and over day after day without conscious thought, never really getting anywhere! I was forced to stop living my life out of habit and without intention.

I have always been one to believe that all things, both good and bad, happen for a reason. Our life circumstances are placed in our path to move us in another direction, a direction with a higher purpose. I was forced to ask myself: What is my higher purpose and why is this happening to me?

At this moment, I decided it was time to make some changes. I made a personal commitment to make a conscious effort to think for myself, to stop acting out of habit, and start acting with intention.

In an effort to escape my physical pain, fear, and anxiety, I decided to attempt to lose all conscious thought through meditation. This deep mediation allowed me to remove my inner (soul) self, from my outer (physical) self. This is where my transformation began.

Five days I spent in this state, disconnected from the physical world and connecting with a deeper, more spiritual, loving world. I connected to a Higher Power. I have connected to Spirit before…but this was different.

From this point forward, life as I knew it was over. I knew there was a higher purpose for my pain and suffering, although at the time I had no clue what that might be, until the morning I awoke, and I knew. I had clarity as to why I went through all that I did.

The burning question I'd had for years was answered. I knew why I was unable to lose those unwanted pounds. The answer was simple: it was NOT *MY* "WHAT"! Yes, it was a goal that I set out to achieve, but it was not my "what"!

What exactly does it mean that weight loss was or is not my "what"? It is my goal, yes, but not my "what." As I mentioned earlier, a "what" is YOUR idea for YOUR future. It is what you desire from the depths of your soul, not what you desire to fit in, to conform to social or societal norms, or to become what others say you should be. Weight loss was not my "what." This was why I was failing to achieve that goal. And it is the reason you are failing to achieve your goal, as well.

The Price of Pursuing Other People's Goals

I recently had a conversation with a friend. She is an empty-nester who has dedicated her life to being a wife and a mommy to her now adult children.

She did a great job. She did everything the way she "thought" she should. She sacrificed her career, her hobbies, her family, and she became the woman society told her she should be. Yet the more she spoke, the more I realized she wasn't happy.

It's a story I hear from so many just like her. Like many other women (and men) who are facing their 50's, she no longer saw her life as endless. She was beginning to feel vulnerable. She no longer felt like she had "all the time in the world." She was starting to feel like "time was running out." It was certainly something I'd been through myself.

Her external persona did not mirror her soul. She no longer knew who she was, what made her happy, what brought her joy, or how she would like to live out the remainder of her life. She expressed some desires for change, but in further conversation, we both came to the realization that those were not *her* desires. They were desires based on the expectations, values, and norms of the society in which she lived. She was paying the price for pursuing other people's goals (OPG) rather than her own personal goals in how depressed and unhappy she felt, her loss of personal identity, and the lack of joy in her life.

Learning To Differentiate Between OPG and MPG

If you take the steps in this book and commit to them, you will embark on a journey of self-discovery like no other. You will gradually open up a part of yourself that you may not yet have met. Your higher self. Your deeper self.

Once you do this, your life will be forever changed. I promise you. No longer will you think on autopilot. You will have intention in all you do and say. You will have control over "YOU."

Unfortunately, many of us have been brainwashed to the point that we no longer think for ourselves. Discovering our "whats" will take some soul searching and perhaps some meditation. If we are to finally achieve our goals, we must first erase the brainwashing and be confident our goals are truly our own, and not those we have been programmed to believe belong to us.

Your goal must be YOUR "what." Not having the ability to differentiate between the two causes emotional havoc as we are not in alignment with our own soul. Years of this misalignment leads to lack of self-worth, addictions, affairs, divorce, depression, and suicide. Others may refer to this stage as the mid-life crisis.

It's Never Too Late

Many people nearing the age of 50 no longer see their lives as endless. We begin to feel vulnerable. We have aches and pains and maybe a diagnosis of a chronic illness. We may have lost one or both parents along with some friends and siblings.

We may begin to feel it's "too late" for us to change, "too late" for us to pursue our dreams, "too late" to make our lives better. Going back to the friend I spoke of earlier, it broke my heart to hear her speak these words, "I can take a job that's easy to kill some time." I asked her if she really wanted to spend the remainder of her life just "killing time."

Our lives are not a dress rehearsal, my friends. Please do not live it out "killing time!" Take the time, do the work, identify what *moves* you, identify your "whats." I am sure I have touched the hearts of many of you "middle-agers" about now.

The good news is that you are not alone, and it is okay! It is never too late to achieve self-awareness. It is never too late to evoke change. It is never too late to lead a happier, more fulfilling life!

Be INSPIRED By Your Goals

As a nurse, I have assisted many patients in developing their goals for change. When working with my clients, I assist them in developing what I refer to as an *INSPIRED* goal. INSPIRED is an acronym I created to ensure the goals my clients set are not only achievable, but desirable.

The acronym stands for *Internal, Needed, Stated, Payoff, Individualized, Related, Evaluable, and Doable.* INSPIRED goals are further discussed below. Along with the development of INSPIRED goals, comes the development of "baby steps." Baby steps are important when working toward goal achievement.

Just as we crawl before we walk, we must reach multiple "micro goals." Micro goals are short-term goals that help us build toward reaching a "macro goal," or long-term goal, that we may have set for ourselves. For each desired change, it is import-ant to have at least one micro goal and one macro goal, as well as a daily plan.

The micro goal is the "baby step" towards your macro goal. Your macro goal is your desired change, your vision of how you desire your life to be. A daily plan is exactly as it states, a plan for the baby steps toward goal achievement you will commit to each day. Your daily plan maps out the baby steps that will move you towards your micro goal, and eventually your macro goal.

Think of it like this: your daily plan is walking, your micro goal is running, and your macro goal is crossing the finish line. Once you have decided upon your goals make sure they are *INSPIRED*. Make sure they pass what I refer to as an "INSPIRED" check. Each goal must have each component listed below:

Internal: *By YOU and for YOU (your "what").* Make sure your "what" (goal) truly belongs to you. We have programmed our subconscious minds based on what we have been told. Therefore, our thoughts may not be owned by us. They may belong to the subconscious programming we have learned from external influences. If we are working towards a goal that we do not internally own, there will be internal resistance, making goal achievement either difficult, or impossible. Make sure your goals are in alignment with your heart and soul's desires.

Needed: *Reasons the change is necessary.* You have identified a need for change (your "why"). Chapter Two focuses on the identification of a "why." "Why's" are your personal reasons as to why change is necessary. Without identification of your reasons for change, it may be challenging to remain focused and on the a forward moving path in the direction towards change.

Stated: *Clearly state your goal.* Your goal ("what") should be clearly stated. For example, "I will lose 5 pounds in one month," as opposed to, "I will lose weight." If your goal is to achieve improved fitness, you would need to take this a step further and be specific as to what this means for you. For example, "I will achieve improved fitness and be able to run two miles 3 days a week without being fatigued, leaving me with the energy required to play with my children and complete my household chores."

Payoff: *What is in it for "YOU?"* What will you gain by achievement of your goal? The "payoff" is the return on your investment. What will you get out of your efforts? Identify and visualize three ways your life will improve once your goals have been met. How does that *feel?*

Individualized: *Tailored to fit YOU.* When developing goals, be sure this goal fits YOUR lifestyle. The "How's" are the steps you have identified and decided to take in the direction of achievement both your micro and macro goals. Your "how" should be in alignment with your needs and lifestyle. Chapter Three focuses on identification of your "hows."

Related: *Related to your "whats."* A goal must be related to the "whats" you have identified. Make sure your goals are related to achieving your desired result. For example, if your "what" is to lose 50 pounds in one year, your micro goals and your Daily Action Plan should reflect this in baby steps. Be mindful that baby steps will get you to your destination.

Evaluable: Evaluate your progress. It is important to set goals in which you are able to evaluate whether or not they have been achieved. Evaluation of achievement is required in order to track your success. For example, it is possible to evaluate a desired 5 pound weight loss goal by a measurable decrease in weight from 150 to 145 pounds. Smoking cessation can also be evaluated, either you smoke, or you don't.

Doable: Your goal ("what" must be doable for YOU. In order to be successful, we must create attainable goals for ourselves. For example, if one were to state their goal, "I will lose 30 pounds in 28 days," statistically speaking, it would be highly unlikely this goal would be reached. In most instances a goal such as this would not be achievable. Always set yourelf up for success!

Identifying The Causes

When setting goals, or identifying our "whats," people often think about changing habits to achieve results such as weight loss, financial security, fitness, or sobriety. When searching your soul for your "what," keep in mind that a goal may be a new, or an improved, relationship. Perhaps you have a history of poor communication, or "angry outbursts," that are hindering achievement of emotionally satisfying intimate relationships. Take time to identify the "root cause" of your behavior.

Are your outbursts learned behaviors that have become a habitual reaction to a trigger? Identification of the source of your habits and behaviors is a crucial element in the change process. If we understand why we are acting, re-acting or behaving in a given manner, we become self-aware. Self-awareness is paramount in the evocation of change.

Why Self-Awareness Matters

What exactly is self-awareness, and why is it so important in evoking changes that result in living the best life possible? Self-awareness is the ability to clearly perceive who you are, including your strengths, weaknesses, thoughts, beliefs, motivations, and emotions. Self-awareness allows you to understand other people, how they perceive you, your attitude, and your responses to them in the moment.

Self-awareness is the first step in creating what you desire. It is the first step toward taking control of your life. The idea behind self-awareness is that where one focuses their thoughts, attention, emotions, and behaviors, determines the outcome of one's life.

Achieving self-awareness allows you to be mindful of exactly where your thoughts and emotions are taking you, thus providing you the ability to take control of those thoughts, emotions, and behaviors, finally making desired changes in your life. The absence of awareness of your thoughts, emotions, words, actions, and behaviors, will result in difficulty making the changes necessary to create permanent behavioral change, and the ability of living the life you desire.

Creating A Daily Plan For Success

Let's talk a bit more about the difference between a micro goal, a macro goal, and a daily plan. As I mentioned earlier, micro goals are the baby steps that are necessary to take in order to reach your macro goal.

Why are baby steps important? Think of it like this: everything in life is a progression of measurable increments. We are born before we die, we walk before we run. Not taking "steps" can make it impossible to progress. It is much easier to take one step at a time up the ladder, than it is to attempt to jump to the top of the ladder from the ground! Don't allow yourself to fall!

In the RONs, a micro goal is an INSPIRED goal we set for ourselves to achieve in 28 days. A macro goal is an INSPIRED goal we set ourselves to achieve over a longer period of time, for example, in one year; it is our vision of desired change. A daily plan is exactly that. It is your plan for the day. The steps are you choosing to take each day to move you in the direction of success, one day at a time.-

An example of a micro goal looks like this, "I will be able to run one mile without feeling tired or short of breath in 28 days." Mark the date on your calendar. Be specific! For example, your daily plan for progression towards this micro goal may look something like this, "today I will commit myself to running/walking once around the block."

It is important that one be specific. Have you ever heard the saying, "If you don't know where you are going, all roads will get you there?" Know where you are going, decide your path, and move forward on that path in the direction of change.

Why mark the date on your calendar? Writing the date on your calendar creates a written, visual remainder of the commitment you have made to yourself. It is important that you honor your commitments to yourself above all others. Be a man or woman of your word, not just to others, but to yourself! You are "numero uno!"

> ## DAILY AFFIRMATION:
> ### *"With each new day comes new strength and new thoughts."*
> *Kathlyn Heim*

Example One: Let's say your goal is weight loss. Weight loss does not pass the INSPIRED check. The effective way to write your macro goal would look similar to the following, "I will reach my weight loss goal of 50 lbs. in one year by (date)."

A micro goal (baby-step) would look more like this, "I will lose 5 lbs. in 28 days by (date)." Again, your daily plan will be your intentional plan for the day. For example, "Today I will eat with intent to nourish my body. I will be conscious of what passes my lips. I will resist temptation of any food(s) that will not support my goal." Don't forget to mark both dates on your calendar!

Example Two: Suppose your goal is to attain financial freedom. Be specific! What exactly does financial freedom mean to you?

For example, a potential macro-goal for financial freedom may look like this, "I will have decreased my spending and saved $2400 in one year by (date)." A micro-goal (baby step) would look like this, "I will have saved $200 in the next 28 days by (date)."

A daily plan for this goal might look something like this, "Today I will act with intention towards achievement of my goal. I will think before making a purchase and ask myself if it is necessary." And of course, this date is marked on your calendar.

Example Three: Let's say you have the goal of abstinence from alcohol or smoking. Your macro goal may be, "I will not consume any alcoholic beverages or cigarettes for one year by (date). "Your micro goal will look like this, "I will not consume any alcoholic beverages for 28 days by (date)," or, "I will not smoke any cigarettes for 28 days by (date)."

And finally, your daily plan may be similar to the following, "Today I will act with intention. Today I will abstain from consumption of any beverages containing alcohol," or "Today I will not smoke any cigarettes." Mark your dates and celebrate your success!

Goals: Your "Whats"
(Write them down each morning, read them each evening)
Identifying Your "Whats" (As many or as few as you choose)

Keeping Track:
For each "what," set a target date and mark it on your calendar. Every 28 days, re-evaluate and set a new goal. WHY? Even though you are creating a 28-day goal, it is important to take things ONE DAY AT A TIME!

_____

_____

_____

_____

_____

_____

_____

_____

_____

_____

_____

_____

_____

Rule 2.

DEFINE YOUR "WHY?"

For every goal you set, ask yourself two questions. Question one, "Why do I desire to achieve this goal?" Question two, "On a scale of 0-10, with 10 being the most important and 0 being not important at all, how important is this goal to me?"

Your "Why" Is What Drives You!

For every "what," there must be a "why." For example, if your goal is to lose 50 pounds, run a marathon, or seek a promotion, you must first know your "why." This requires some deep thinking, again, perhaps coupled with some prayer or meditation, depending on your spirituality or belief system.

Is your goal to achieve improved health, income, or prestige? If yes, be specific. What does improved health mean to you? Do you have a diagnosis of Hypertension or Type II Diabetes Mellitus, or are you simply overweight or low on energy?

Let's say your goal is to have $2400 in the bank within one year. Why? Is it to take a vacation? Is it to provide a financial cushion in order to decrease your anxiety and improve sleep lost over worry at night?

Perhaps your goal is a new, or an improved, relationship. Again, ask yourself "*why?*" If you are not able to identify your "why," it may be difficult to stay focused.

If you are unable to identify your "whys," it may be difficult to move forward. Your "whys" make it possible to act with intention. Each time you make a decision to act, or not act, you must be mindful as to "why."

How Important Is This Goal To You?

How important is the achievement of this goal to YOU? Keep in mind, if your desired goal carries the importance of a 2 on a 0-10 scale, perhaps it is not that important to you, and maybe some soul-searching will help you discover a more meaningful goal.

List Three Reasons Why

Sit down with a pen and your journal. At the top of the page write, "3 Reasons Why This Goal (or desired change of behavior) Is Important To Me." Next, spend ten minutes writing, without stopping the pen or reflecting on it, as to why it matters to you that this goal is achieved.

When you're done, highlight each of the reasons that you found, and rate them according to the scale provided above. Circle the three most important reasons that you discover in this exercise. You may be surprised at the answers.

Listing reasons for achievement can be helpful in discerning whether this goal is truly one that belongs to you, or whether it comes from someone else. If it is YOUR goal, and it's important YOU, move forward with it. If it's a goal that belongs to someone other than yourself, discard it.

Keep Your Eyes On The "Whys"

I encourage you to write down, and carry with you, a list of your "whys." Place your list in your wallet, your lunchbox, the dash of your car, anywhere that is repeatedly visible to you. The more you acknowledge and reinforce your "whys," the more likely you are to think before you act. You begin making conscious, not subconscious, decisions.

Keep in mind that it is your "whys" that *drive* you. It is your "whys" that *inspire* you to act. In order to live a life with intention, you must consider your "whys" with any and all of your actions. "Whys" are individual and subjective.

Living a life out of habit eliminates the purpose and motivation for acting. This causes you to exist, rather than live a life with purpose or meaning. Would you agree that the majority of us desire to live a life of purpose? The feeling or belief that we are merely existing, living a life without purpose, can lead to depression, addictions, failed relationships, job dissatisfaction, disease, and suicide.

Knowing "Why" Restores Our Joy

Recently, I had a conversation with a co-worker. I will call her Mary. She expressed unhappiness and discontent with her job as a nurse care manager. She was unable to identify the "whys," or the purpose, of her role. She felt that day in and day out she put an exorbitant amount of energy into providing her patients with the education necessary to improve their health outcomes. She expressed that she felt this to be a "waste of time," as "they don't listen," and "do what they want anyway."

"Why do they even have care managers?" she asked.

After listening to her express her thoughts and frustrations, I asked her for permission to share some information with her. I shared with her the concept of identifying a person's "whats," "whys," and "hows."

I encouraged her to speak with her patients about identifying what exactly they would like to happen. What is their final goal? Once the patient's final goal is identified, inquire as to what their "whys" are. Why do they desire a particular outcome? Then discuss with them how they believe they will be able to achieve this outcome.

Finally, I encouraged her to have her patients create a list of the "payoffs," the return on their "investment." What is in it for them? How will their life/situation/health improve when they achieve their desired result or goal? A payoff is based on an internal reward system, therefore personal to them only. Keep in mind, external reward systems are unreliable. Payoffs will be discussed in detail in Chapter Four.

I continued the conversation, yet switched my focus away from the patient and towards my co-worker. She had expressed discontent and was feeling as if her role as a care manager was without purpose. I encouraged her to self-reflect as to why she became a nurse, why she became a care manager, and why she chooses to remain employed in this position.

After some thought, Mary responded. She shared with me that she became a nurse to fulfill her life-long desire to help others. She transitioned into her role as a care manager, as the schedule afforded her more time with her family, as well as an increase in income. When asked, Mary stated that a schedule conducive to spending time with her family, and increased income, is her "what."

When asked "why," Mary stated that the increased income allows her to take trips and partake in family activities, and the schedule allows her the time to do so. Suddenly Mary's face lit up and she smiled. "Oh Kathlyn, I get it now, thank you. This is not a waste of time. My purpose to come to work is not only to help others; it is so I can live the life I want also!!

Two weeks later Mary stopped by my desk and thanked me again. She told me that our conversation was a pivotal point of change in her life. Each morning when her alarm wakes her, she has a smile in her heart as she knows there is purpose as to why she is in her current place of employment. She no longer feels there is no purpose in her career.

She feels satisfied that her career allows her to live her life as she chooses. Her payoff is the joy and happiness she feels when spending quality time with her family. Mary also expressed that she has been discussing with her patients their "whats" and "whys," discovering that this personalization has caused some of them to begin making the changes necessary to improve their health outcomes.

As Mary has learned, if we are able to identify our "whys," we automatically gain a sense of purpose behind our actions, followed by the feeling of living a purposeful life.

DAILY AFFIRMATION:
"The best way to achieve success tomorrow is to prepare today."
Kathlyn Heim

Identify 3 "Whys" for each "What"

_____

_____

_____

_____

_____

_____

_____

_____

_____

_____

_____

_____

_____

_____

_____

_____

_____

_____

Rule 3.

CHOOSE YOUR "HOWS"

The "hows" are the steps you have identified and decided to take in the direction of achieving both your micro and macro goals. For each micro goal, you will list 3 baby steps you will take in order to achieve it. Again, be specific!

3 Steps A Day Per Goal

In the creation of your goals, do not simply state, "I will lose 5 lbs. in 28 days by eating healthier, exercising, and drinking more water." Again, put pen to paper in your journal, and define what this means to you specifically. For example, "I will lose 5 lbs. in 28 days by taking the following 3 steps:

1. I will keep a daily log of my caloric intake, and limit total calories to 1200 per day, eliminate sugar and processed foods, and eat 16 ounces of lean protein and 6 servings of vegetables, and 3 servings of grains divided into 4 small meals daily.

2. I will get 30 minutes of cardio activity (walking or swimming) 5 times a week.
3. I will drink 80 ounces of water daily.

If your goal is to break the habit of irresponsible spending, and save $2400 in one year, this will require you to take daily steps towards this goal. You must be in agreement that these steps are achievable and will fit comfortably into your lifestyle.

For example:

1. I will not make any unnecessary purchases including clothes, food, entertainment, or otherwise.
2. I will work 4 hours of overtime every Monday.
3. I will be mindful to turn lights off and limit the unnecessary use of electrical appliances to cut back on the money I spend on my electric bill.

Let's say your goal is to "get over" a past relationship in 6 months. Your daily action plan may look something like this:

1. Today I will not call my ex (unless it is a bad name, LOL)
2. Today I will not stalk my ex on social media.
3. Today I will perform one act of self-love.

When formulating your "hows," be sure to agree to them. If your "hows" do not fit into your lifestyle, or are not something you are willing to do, you will need to rethink them. Once you have decided upon your "hows," put them into action with your Daily Action Plan. Decide each morning the baby steps you will be taking towards goal achievement.

Including Your "Hows" In Your Daily Plan

Each morning you will include your "hows" in your daily plan. For example, "Today I will act with intention to achieve my desired weight loss goal. Today I will keep a log of my caloric intake, walk 10,000 steps, and consume 8 glasses of water."

Commit Each Day

Be aware that we most certainly will meet temptation! Life has a way of getting in the way. Things will happen that will pull you away from your daily action plan. Commit to seeing it through, regardless of the bumps in the road, this is life!

Successful goal achievement is not about perfection, it is about commitment. Have you ever heard the saying, "It is not what you eat from November to January, it is what you eat from January to November?"

There is a lot of truth to that statement. Learn to focus on the bigger picture. Mark each day that you have remained committed to your daily action plan, with a star on your calendar. Learn to let go and stop focusing on the one moment that you were human, and lost a battle with temptation!

Change takes commitment, consistency, and time. We live in what I refer to as a "fast food world." We have become accustomed to instant gratification, expecting instant results. This concept does not only apply to food, it can be applied in most areas of our lives, including dating. Stay tuned in for my next book, "Dating in a Fast Food World: A Girlfriend's Guide to Internet Dating," which delves into this phenomenon.

It is my belief that the saturation of online dating, shopping and porn, as well as social media sites, have contributed to the mindset that we must receive results instantaneously. Keep in mind, although easy access has become our norm, most things that provide intrinsic rewards require time.

One cannot achieve a college degree instantaneously. Strong, healthy, lasting relationships develop over years, not minutes.

Building a savings account, pension, or retirement fund takes years. Again, be patient, be consistent, and be committed to your "whats." You've got this!!

Re-Evaluating And Adjusting

Daily steps will be re-evaluated every 28 days. Why re-evaluate? In order to ensure success in achieving your macro goals, ask yourself, "Did this work? Is there something more, or more effective, I could be doing? Are my "hows" fitting into my lifestyle?"

Why "Winging It" Doesn't Work

I had a client who desired to lose weight. She had the macro goal of losing 100 lbs. by the end of the year and it was February, so it was an INSPIRED goal. She had identified her "what" and her "whys." After several months of yo-yo dieting, she had not lost any weight.

The problem was that my client had not identified her "hows." She was missing a crucial step necessary for success. Each day she "winged it." She didn't have a clear plan on how she would reach her weight loss goal.

I worked with her on development of her "hows," as well as journaling her daily plan. She decided her "hows" included meal preparation each Sunday, walking for 30 minutes on her lunch break, and keeping a food diary. Each morning, she journaled positive affirmations, read her goals, and spent time in meditation. Each morning, she had a plan for the day and committed herself to following that plan.

What do you think happened? You guessed it. She began to experience results! I am happy to share that she is now 50lbs closer to her weight loss goal of 100lbs! She followed the steps to success. She admits that she no longer has to "think" as much about what she is going to do each day. Her plan has now become her habit and her new way of living.

When Things Go Wrong

As humans, we are less than perfect. Life is not perfect, and things do not always go as planned. There may be unplanned circumstances that are out of our control and prevent us from "sticking" to our daily plan of action. Or, perhaps we got off track for a moment and it had nothing at all to do with external circumstances.

It is not uncommon to have what are called 'triggers' that lead us to our old way of thinking or acting. Maybe you had an argument with your significant other and "ate the cake," or "drank the drink," without giving it any thought, acting purely out of habit. Or, perhaps you did give it thought, but at that moment in time you "didn't give a s#@t" about your daily plan or your goals for that matter.

Perhaps you went back to your old lover…for just one night! Relax, take a deep breath, acknowledge what has just occurred, identify your trigger, let it go, and move forward! When things don't go as planned, do not give up.

For example, have you ever been on a weight loss diet and "cheated?" You may have let that one moment in time that you "ate the cake," lead you to throw the diet out the window for the rest of the day, week, or month. You then kept eating foods that took you further away vs. closer to your goal.

This is a common practice for many people and involves "all-or-nothing" thinking. This all-or-nothing thinking can be very destructive, taking a toll on our self-confidence and self-worth. It often causes us to emotionally "beat ourselves up," resulting in the inability to move forward towards successful goal achievement.

This is when we begin to participate in self-sabotaging behaviors. Self-sabotaging behaviors will be discussed further in Chapter 9. For now, we will discuss how to move away from this all-or-nothing way of thinking. Focus on your successes. If you've been marking the days you committed on your calendar, go and look at those. Remind yourself of how many days you succeeded.

Let your so-called failures be your teacher. Let them prompt you to explore the "root cause" of your actions. This will result in a deepening level of self-awareness, and an increased ability to act with intention.

If you are able to fully understand why you are acting or behaving in a particular manner, you will be more aware of the causes and triggers, and thus will be able to make a conscious decision about whether or not you will perform that particular act or behavior in the future.

When things do not go as planned, do not give up! If you were driving to a particular destination and took a wrong turn would you say, "What the heck, I guess I will just go this way," and continue in the wrong direction? Of course not! You would stop, read your directions, and get on the road that leads to your destination!

Do not let one incident, or one "slip up," prevent you from moving forward towards success! Focus on the big picture. Stay committed to your "whats." Be patient.

> DAILY AFFIRMATION:
> *"Today I am thankful for the ability to make my own choices."*
> Kathlyn Heim

Identify Your 3 "Hows"

_____

_____

_____

_____

_____

_____

_____

_____

_____

_____

_____

_____

_____

_____

_____

_____

九

Section II:

THE NEXT THREE RULES

Rule 4.

IDENTIFY YOUR PAYOFFS

L et's recap. You have identified your "whats," "whys," and "hows." Now it is time to identify your "payoffs."

Getting A Return On Your Investment

What is a "payoff"? A "payoff" is the return on your investment. It is what you will get out of your efforts. Identify and visualize three ways your life will be different if you achieve your goal. How does that *feel?*

For example, "If I save $2,400 in one year, I will have the financial freedom to make a purchase or take trips with my family."

This will improve my life by:

1. Allowing me to take my family on a Caribbean cruise (and post pics on social media #haters #EatYourHeartOut #DontBeJealous).

2. Allowing me to invest in my retirement fund, decreasing worry and anxiety over the future.

3. Allowing me to purchase gifts for my friends and family during the holidays without accumulating additional debt.

Choosing The Right Payoffs

A "payoff" must be based on an intrinsic, or internal, reward system. Intrinsic reward systems are intangible, meaning you can't touch them. They include rewards like health, happiness, joy, peace, memories, self-confidence, self-achievement, and self-love, among others. They cannot be removed by someone or something.

Intrinsic rewards are not dependent upon external factors and, therefore, they cannot be "taken away." Intrinsic rewards provide a person with a sense of meaning and purpose or importance for achieving the goal you are striving to accomplish. These feelings of meaning and purpose stem from the belief that your commitment and efforts are worth your time and energy.

On the other hand, we have what is referred to as extrinsic or external reward systems. Extrinsic reward systems involve approval, money, status, the list goes on. Because extrinsic reward systems are tangible, they do not come from within a person, and are provided *to* the person exhibiting the behavior from an outside source.

Extrinsic reward systems can be eradicated without warning, for reasons outside of our control. In recap, internal rewards come from within the person, external reward systems come from something outside the person.

What Motivates Us

Let's take this a step further and talk about motivation for change. Extrinsic, or external motivation, occurs when we are motivated to perform a particular behavior or act, that will result in receiving a reward, or to avoid a negative consequence. In this circumstance, the behavior or act in which you engage is either to receive some type of reward, or to avoid a negative consequence. An example of extrinsic motivation would be participation in a sporting event in order to win a trophy.

Intrinsic, or internal motivation, involves performing a particular behavior or act because it is personally rewarding. An example of intrinsic motivation would be participation in a sporting event, not to receive a trophy, but because you find the activity enjoyable.

As you may have concluded, *intrinsic motivation* involves a much deeper, internal motivation. An example of intrinsic motivation would be a Nurse Care Manager who is driven by improving the health and lives of others. Intrinsic motivation stems from the meaning and purpose behind your behaviors and actions. This meaning and purpose drives your behavior, regardless of any external reward or compensation.

It is important that while identifying our "whats," we choose those that intrinsically motivate us. As I pointed out earlier, an internal reward system is not only powerful, it cannot be influenced or eradicated by someone, something, or a circumstance.

I recently watched a YouTube video of a popular author and motivational speaker, who will remain nameless. He was speaking to his viewers about the importance of a positive reward system in order to achieve success and change. He gave the example of rewarding yourself after completing an act that you find difficult or do not like to do.

His example was as follows: If you do not like to exercise, and are attempting to make exercise part of your daily routine, each time you go to the gym, reward yourself with something you do like. He suggested chocolate.

I don't know about you, but if I want chocolate, I will eat chocolate regardless of whether or not I go to the gym! Consuming chocolate after performing a desired act provides an external reward system and lacks power and sustainability. On the other hand, let's look at the same activity performed, working out, with the payoff being based on an internal reward system.

If a person has the goal of daily exercise, have them identify their internal "payoff," for example, the feeling of self-confidence, achievement, or success. It is those powerful internal rewards, or "payoffs," that will enable an individual to achieve success.

Visualize The Payoffs

Now, imagine yourself having achieved your desired goal. How does this *feel?* Close your eyes and visualize yourself in this position. Do you feel happy, relieved, accomplished, successful, empowered, thankful, or motivated? Do you see where I am going with this?

Visualization is a technique used by many successful people, including professional athletes and entrepreneurs of large, successful companies. Visualization involves the use of your imagination to paint a picture in your mind of what your life will be like when your goals are achieved.

Visualization allows us to activate our subconscious mind and begin acting toward our desired goals in the absence of conscious thought. Visualization assists in replacing unwanted habits, thoughts, and behaviors with those which we desire.

Have you heard of the concept, "watch your thoughts as they become words, watch your words as they become actions, watch your actions as they become your destiny?" That is the truth my friends…think about it and you will see it become a reality!

The Power of Payoffs

A client of mine, let's call him Bob, just hated to work out. He was in his mid-fifties, had lost some muscle tone, and found some extra "fluff." Together, we worked through the steps in the RON's.

Bob identified that his "what" was to get in "better physical shape." More specifically, Bob desired to lose 20lbs, and regain muscle tone and size. He identified his "whys," which included improved physical appearance, an increase in energy, and improved health.

Bob's "hows" included daily physical exercise, elimination of processed foods, and limiting consumption of beer to the weekends. During the visualization exercise, Bob was able to identify his "payoffs," his internal rewards for achievement of his goal of improving his physical shape. Bob stated his payoff would be an increase in self-confidence, which he had somehow lost along the way.

Bob made a commitment to follow the principles of the RONs. I am happy to announce that Bob not only achieved his goal, he admits that his gym routine has become a "habit." He looks forward to his daily visit to the gym. He believes his improved physical appearance and increase in self-confidence were influential in his recent promotion at his place of employment. Congratulations, Bob! It makes me happy to share in your success, which is *my* internal "payoff" for living my life purpose.

Identification of the "payoff" is a crucial step in successful goal achievement. In life, the majority of our actions are motivated by payoffs. We work to receive a paycheck. We eat to satisfy hunger. As previously mentioned, the payoff for goal achievement must be based on an internal reward system.

I would like to share another story as to how the identification of the "whys" and "payoffs" lead a client of mine towards successful goal achievement. My client, whom for privacy purposes I will call Megan, expressed to me that she desired to further her education by obtaining an advanced college degree. This was her "what." On the scale of 0-10, her desire was a 10.

I asked her this question, "If your desire to obtain this degree is a 10/10, what is preventing you from returning to school?" Megan began to answer with her "why nots." When she finished with all her reasons why she has not moved forward with her goal, I asked her to take a few minutes to reflect, and think about her "whys."

I asked her to give me three reasons *why* she would obtain her advanced degree. After just a couple of minutes, Megan was able to tell me three reasons she desired to continue her education. Megan had identified her "whys."

I then asked her to close her eyes and visualize how her life would be different once she obtained her advanced degree. "Visualize yourself walking across the stage with your diploma at your graduation. Your friends and family are all in attendance. How does this *feel?*" I asked.

Finally, I asked her, "What is your 'payoff?' What internal reward will you receive upon achievement of this goal? With a smile on her face, Megan was able to express to me how her family's life, and her life, would be improved upon achievement of this goal. Just two weeks after our session, Megan was proud to disclose to me she had enrolled in two online college courses. Way to go Megan!!

TODAY'S AFFIRMATION:
"Allow your dreams to become your destiny."
Kathlyn Heim

Identify your 3 "Payoffs"

_____

_____

_____

_____

_____

_____

_____

_____

_____

_____

_____

_____

_____

_____

_____

_____

_____

Rule 5.

DECLUTTER
YOUR LIFE

Prior to embarking upon your journey toward change, it is important that you declutter your life and your mind. What does it mean to declutter your life and mind? Have you ever heard the saying, "out with the old and in with the new?" This is the concept we are applying.

Making Room For The New

In order to move forward and make room for the "new" we must first get rid of the "old." What is it that is currently weighing you down? Wouldn't it feel great to lose that extra weight or baggage?

The concept of "decluttering" came to me from a personal friend, who is a successful and intelligent woman, the CEO and founder of her company, a business owner, and an author. More important, this amazing woman has struggled with addiction and, at the time I am writing this book, is celebrating 14 years in recovery.

She spoke to me about throw rugs she had in her hallway. Day in and day out the rugs bothered her. They were cluttering her personal space. This clutter was blocking her creativity and hindering her productivity.

One day, she decided to remove them from her hallway. Doing so uncluttered her personal space and allowed her to "open up" and make room for peace.

Declutter Your Personal Space

First, you must declutter your personal space. Remove everything in your physical space that is occupying time in your mind. How are you going to cook if all the dishes are dirty and in the sink? Take some time to think about what in your personal space is distracting you from moving forward.

How will you remove these distractions? Visualize how you will feel when those distractions are removed. Will you have peace or clarity? Will you feel more invigorated and motivated?

Declutter Your Mental Space

Once you have decluttered your personal space, it is time to declutter your emotional, or "mind space." Once you determine exactly what is occupying space in your mind and thoughts, you must then determine just how much space this clutter is occupying.

When it comes to "mind space," rent is not cheap. There is a high price you are paying! Do you have past relationships, hurts, disappointments, or insecurities that are renting valuable space in your mind? Think of your mind like a glass. If your glass is full of what you don't want to drink, how will you be able to fill it with something you do want to drink?

Ask yourself, "How full is my glass?" Now determine what needs to be emptied from your glass in order to fill it with something more desirable. You may be thinking, "Ok, sounds good, but how do I do this? How do I evict this 'clutter' from renting valuable space in my mind?" We're going to talk about that next.

Identify Your Thoughts

The first step in removing clutter from your mind is identification. Identify what it is that is occupying your thoughts and not allowing room for new ways of thinking. Again, I will remind you, "watch your thoughts as they become words, watch your words as they become actions, watch your actions as they become your destiny." Once you have identified your renters, acknowledge them, and write them down in your journal.

Feel Your Feelings

A lot of what occupies our mind space are feelings. Unprocessed feelings of hurt, sadness, emotional pain, rejection, and failure are common mental occupants and can take up a lot of space.

Your feelings exist to communicate to you something important about your environment or your life that you need to know. Each one has a message to bring you, but if you don't allow yourself to experience those feelings, you won't get those messages.

Let yourself feel them. Keep in mind that feelings need only be visitors, not permanent tenants.

DAILY AFFIRMATIONS:
*"Feelings are visitors, let them come
and let them go."*
Kathlyn Heim

Acknowledge And Let Go

Like most of you, there have been many times in life I have found my mind space invaded by unwelcome occupants. It is my practice to quickly "kick them out!" through daily mediation.

One can meditate on their own or listen to a variety of guided meditations found on YouTube.

In meditations in which I am attempting to release feelings, I visualize writing them down and sending them up into the air in a balloon or sending them floating down a slow-moving river. I visualize myself watching them until they are no longer visible.

Acknowledge your feelings, validate them, then LET THEM GO! Below is a poem I wrote that may help you with this "letting go" process.

Feelings

Feelings
Friends,
Enemies.
Our biggest strength,
Or strongest weakness.
Valid,
Invalid.
The precursor of hate,
And of love.
The beginning,
Or the end.
They breed life,
And end life.
The reason we laugh, cry, fail, succeed.
Nonexistent to the five senses,

Yet stronger than all combined.
Feelings are just visitors,
Let them come,
Then let them go.

Perform An Act Of Release

Letting go may sound easy, but often it isn't. That's why I recommend you perform an act of release to help you with the letting go process. What does this mean?

The act of letting go can be performed mentally via meditation or conscious thought as described above, or through a physical action. An example of this physical act of release would be writing your undesirable feelings down on paper and then burning them or putting them in a balloon and sending them away. Throw them in a river or the ocean and watch them drift away.

I am going to share another personal experience to better help you understand how to perform an act of release. After experiencing the "break up" of a relationship, I was left feeling hurt and empty. I found myself struggling to move forward with my life. Negative emotions, feelings, and thoughts were occupying valuable space in my mind, preventing me from having room for more positive thoughts, and moving forward with my life.

I decided to perform several acts of release. I rode a bike for a long distance and visualized leaving my prior lover and all the attached negative emotions behind me, while visualizing a new relationship and positive, loving, happy thoughts on the horizon at my destination. In simple terms, I visualized leaving the past behind me, and moving forward to the future I desired.

Identify What Needs To Be Decluttered In Your Physical Space

_____

_____

_____

_____

_____

_____

_____

Identify What Needs To Be Decluttered In Your Mental Space

_____

_____

_____

_____

_____

_____

_____

Rule 6.

OVERCOME BARRIERS

What exactly is a barrier? A barrier is anything that potentially prevents you from achieving your goal(s).

Barriers Are Part of Life

A barrier can be a person, place, thing, or circumstance. It is highly likely that these barriers are what have prevented you from achieving success in the past. I will provide a list of potential barriers at the end of this chapter.

Steps To Removing Barriers

The first step in removing a barrier is identification and acknowledgment of the barrier's existence. Sound familiar? We are getting "real" here.

The second step is formulating solutions for overcoming these barriers. Think of a barrier as more of a roadblock. Roadblocks are meant to be removed!

Suppose one of your commitment steps is to drink 80 ounces of water a day (not spiked!), but you don't like water. Your distaste for water is a potential barrier to your success.

You brainstorm solutions to remove this barrier and continue achieving your goals. Perhaps you can add things like cucumber, lemon, lime, or mint sprigs to give your water a more pleasant taste. You overcame the barrier and you are now able to continue on your way towards the goal of a healthier body.

If You Can't Remove The Barrier, Find A Different Route!

However, let's say that your solution doesn't work. You re-evaluate 28 days later and you realize that your distaste for water is still keeping you from achieving your goals. It's time to come up with a more realistic step for you.

Remember, you are not setting yourself up for failure. You are the one and only person who is able to set yourself up for success! YOU know the way, YOU have the skills, and YOU are able to make this happen!

People Can Be Barriers, Too

Keep in mind that barriers are not limited to situations or circumstances. People can also be a barrier to your success.

I highly recommend you take a look at the people you choose to allow in your life and personal space. Be mindful of their influence. I am not one to view any situation as "black or white." However, if the people in your life are not your teammate, they may be your opponent.

What exactly does that mean? If we do not carefully choose who is in our lives, we may inadvertently allow others to occupy both our mental and physical space.

Do you have any toxic people in your life that are preventing you from achieving your goals? Are they over-demanding of your time, your emotions, and your thoughts? Are they sabotaging your efforts?

Are these people preventing you from following your daily plan? Are they adding value to your life, or are they taking it away? Take time to evaluate and remember to "take care of YOU first!"

True Confessions Of A Human Barrier

I have a funny personal story to share. Earlier in the book I shared with you my life-long struggle to lose weight. Well, I hate to admit it, but this inability to lose weight caused me to do some not-so-nice things. My best friend at the time, we were 15, was what we now call a skinny bitch.

No, she wasn't a bitch in the true sense of the word, she was just skinny, and she didn't have to try…bitch! Lol. One Halloween, my green eyes and jealous bones got the best of me. After miles of trick-or-treating on roller skates, we obtained an exorbitant amount of candy, including lots of chocolate. I decided to give my friend all of my candy.

Why would I do this? The answer: to make her fat! You see, she loved candy. Well, my efforts to sabotage her did not work. She ate the candy, but she did not get fat. In fact, I don't think she gained an ounce. She did get some pretty bad acne from the chocolate, though she was still beautiful inside and out.

Shame on me…I was a barrier. I was a sabotager. I would NEVER do something like this again…Karma is the real bitch! However, the point I am trying to make is that sometimes people around you can get jealous of your success and will try to sabotage you. They can allow their jealousy to turn them into a barrier.

Examples of Potential Barriers And How To Remove Them

Goal: Dietary changes for improved nutrition/health.

Barrier: Lack of knowledge on the nutritional content of foods.

Plan: Obtain educational materials from a reliable source as to what your personal nutritional requirements are.

Goal: Abstinence from alcohol.

Barrier: Your favorite "watering hole" you pass on the way from work to home.

Plan: Take a different route home or make a commitment to meet a friend at the gym, thus creating healthy habits.

Goal: Weight loss.

Barrier: Your girlfriend, who is jealous that you have lost some weight, is attempting to sabotage your efforts by surprising you with a Mocha Frappuccino and your favorite pastry or is having an "emotional crisis" that only you can solve during your scheduled workout.

Plan: Revert to your daily plan and stick to it! Schedule your workout, meditations and journaling in your calendar and DO NOT CHANGE YOUR DAILY PLAN! Politely schedule time for this friend when it convenient for you. If your girlfriend takes offense, she is not your teammate, she is your opponent. You will need to re-evaluate her presence in your life. (#cutthefat "How To Recognize and Eliminate Toxic People From Your Life," another of my upcoming book titles.)

DAILY AFFIRMATION:
"I possess within me the power and the strength to achieve all that I set my mind to."
Kathlyn Heim

Identify Potential Barriers

_____

_____

_____

_____

_____

_____

_____

Strategies For Removing Your Barriers

_____

_____

_____

_____

_____

_____

_____

Develop an "Action Plan"

_____

_____

_____

_____

_____

_____

_____

_____

_____

_____

_____

_____

_____

_____

_____

_____

_____

_____

九

Section III:

THE FINAL THREE RULES

Rule 7.

REPLACE OLD HABITS

When you understand how neural pathways are created in the brain, you will gain an understanding of how to let go of old habits and create new ones. This will allow you to become successful in creating change.

Neural Pathways & Their Role in Change

I like to think of neural pathways as deep, fast-flowing rivers of nerve cells that transmit messages to the brain. The longer and faster the river flows, the deeper it becomes. As it relates to the human mind, the more one exhibits a specific behavior, the deeper the neural, or "brain," pathway becomes, thus creating what is known as a habit.

For example, a person may reach for a cigarette, a drink, or a comfort food when they become stressed. The more often the person performs this act or habit, the more embedded the habit becomes, forming a deeper neural pathway. The deeper the neural pathway becomes, the harder the habit is to change.

A Scientific Approach To "Kicking the Habit"

The good news is these neural pathways can be changed! We *are* in control of our actions. Creating new actions will create new neural pathways and new habits. This is what is called the neuroplasticity of the brain.

The more we exercise our new habit, the deeper the new neural pathway becomes. The process of creating new neural pathways takes approximately 28 days. Let me explain what this means to you and why this is so important when attempting to make behavioral changes.

For example, when I was asked how I put on my shoes, I was unable to answer. Putting on my shoes was a habit. I performed this action multiple times a day for many, many years. I was no longer using my conscious mind to put on my shoes.

My neural pathways were a deep, flowing river. Putting on my shoes was a habit. Of course, as soon as possible, I reached for a pair of shoes to put on in order to become aware of my habits. I put my right shoe on first (Jimmy Choo 4" heel, candy apple red, patent leather of course!), then put on my left shoe.

I decided to test this theory, and intentionally put my shoes on in the opposite order for 28 days. What do you suppose happened? If your answer is that I now put my shoes on left to right without any thought, you are correct! I consciously created new neural pathways in my brain, therefore creating a new, more desirable habit!

I was successful by using intention to re-program my brain to do what "I" wanted it to do. The same holds true for all habits. Although some habits are more challenging than others to break, know that it is possible. You can remove a behavior or thought or addictions directly from the brain. This is science!

When New Habits Take Over

I will speak again about my client who was unsuccessful in her weight loss attempts prior to following the RONs. She completed the recommended steps and was able to erase her old, negative habits that did not support her goals, and replace them with new, healthy habits that are moving her towards success.

When asked, she stated that initially her daily plan took a lot of thought and practice. She felt as if she were continually placing a "STOP" sign in her mind in order to not act (eat) or to act (walk on her lunch) out of habit. She admitted to struggling to remember to be intentional in her actions and follow her daily plan.

Although she is unable to pinpoint when the transition occurred, she now doesn't really have to think about making a healthier choice when it comes to food. As far as her lunchtime walks, she automatically reaches for her walking shoes at lunch break and looks forward to using that time to "declutter" her mind.

> DAILY AFFIRMATION:
> *"Have the courage and the strength to be the best YOU, one day at a time."*
> *Kathlyn Heim*

Rule 8.

ACT WITH INTENTION

Somewhere, at someplace in time, I overheard a conversation about how the brain will talk a person out of action within the first five seconds of the thought. Hmmm... could this be true? Inquiring minds wanted to know.

I definitely have an inquiring mind! What did I do? I put this theory to the test.

Your Lazy Brain

The following morning my alarm went off at 4:00 am. It was time to get up and work out. I will not lie, on most days I would re-set my alarm for 6:00 am, get some extra z's, and head off to work promising myself I would hit the gym after work.

Then, when "after work" came, would anyone care to guess what happened? I thought about working out, but...the more I thought about it, the more I talked myself out of it. I already worked a full day and I had at least a 45-minute commute home. My friends were meeting for happy hour. The football game is on. I need to fold laundry. The grass might need watering. You get my drift?

Tomorrow!! I will wake up at 4:00 am tomorrow and get that workout in, for sure, cross my heart, come rain or shine, I will be there.

What do you suppose happened the following morning at 4:00 am? You guessed it. Repeat, repeat, repeat! Don't get me wrong, I am not bragging about this behavior. I wanted to go to the gym. I knew how working out benefitted me both emotionally and physically.

So why not just get up and go? Simple: I did what most of us do best. I talked myself out of it.

Don't Let More Than 5 Seconds Pass

Getting back to the conversation I heard about the five seconds to act. I decided to try it myself. The following morning when my alarm went off at 4:00 am, I counted down...5-4-3-2-1-GO!

I jumped out of bed, put my gym clothes on, got in the car, and off I went! Although sometimes a struggle, I apply this principle 4 days a week. I no longer allow my brain to talk myself out of action. This action is my commitment to myself, a commitment to my goal of better health and fitness. I am not saying that it is always easy, I just don't let more than five seconds pass when I have a plan of action. Try it!!

Wait Five Seconds

I know what you are thinking. What...wait five seconds to act? You just told me to act within five seconds! Correction, I said to act *within* five seconds of a decision you have already made that was decided on by YOU as a step towards reaching your goal.

Are you confused? Please let me help. Acting with intention is intended to help you through those unplanned situations. For example, your goal involves weight loss, you are at work, and you forgot that lunch you prepared. You know, the spinach with the 3oz of roasted chicken and vinegar dressing.

The food truck pulls up. You are starving. That greasy cheeseburger the slender young woman walked away with looks and smells so good! That's what I want! Not at all fair that she can eat like that and still be a skinny bitch! (Relax, I'm not hating on her, just a figure of speech!). Time to apply the rule, "act with intention," and "wait five seconds."

Party pooper! Again, *please* don't hate on me. I am here to help. I am providing you with tools for success. For five seconds think about your goals. For five seconds think about your daily plan and commitment to yourself. For five seconds think about how important the achievement of your goal is to you.

For five seconds imagine yourself having achieved this goal. How does this *feel?* For five seconds, think about how your life will change upon achievement of those goals. Is it worth it? How important is the success to YOU? And, last, how will you feel if you "give in" to temptation?

Now go home and journal your success. How does it feel passing up that cheeseburger and fries? How do you feel knowing that you ate your spinach salad with the intent to curb your hunger, nourish your body, and move one step closer to your goal? Congratulations! (#yougotthis)

DAILY AFFIRMATION:
"I possess within me the power and strength
to achieve all that I set my mind to."
Kathlyn Heim

Rule 9.

GET OUT OF YOUR OWN WAY

What happens when we have identified our "what" our "why," our "how," our "payoff," and still have not been able to move forward? We know we have a sincere desire to be successful, but for some reason we just can't get out of our own way. I am here to give you some reassurance, you are not alone! This, my friends, is what is known as ambivalence.

Ambivalence: Caught Between the Pros and Cons List

Ambivalence means that you are moving one step closer in the direction towards change. Do not worry. I hear your question without you even asking. What the heck is ambivalence, where did I get it, and how do I get rid of it?

Ambivalence is wanting something, but not wanting to give something up. Ambivalence is being caught between the pros and cons list.

I will give you an example. While implementing my RONs theory, I had a goal of weight loss. I wanted to lose weight, but I wanted to keep my lifestyle "status quo," so to speak. I wanted to have the results of weight loss, yet my love of fine dining and wining was far more important to me than a smaller dress size.

Helping You Spot Goals That Aren't Truly YOUR Goals

Although weight loss had been my to-this-date unachieved life-long goal, the process of implementing the RONs helped me to realize that it really wasn't as important to me as I had previously believed. It was a societal goal that my mind had tricked me into buying into.

I cannot emphasize enough how important it is to work towards goals that are important to YOU, for YOU, rather than goals set by societal norms. If your goal does not truly belong to you, if it does not come from your heart, you may be at risk for being stuck in ambivalence for the rest of eternity. The benefits of change will have to outweigh the cons of giving up life as you know it, before you will be able to achieve the goal.

Addressing Ambivalence

Make a list of pros and cons. What are you losing or giving up, and what are you gaining? What is the benefit? Are you giving up alcohol to achieve sobriety and improve your relationships? Are you giving up chatting with co-workers on your lunch break to achieve inner peace and success in goal achievement?

How comfortable are you with giving up a desired behavior in order to achieve your goal? How important is sustaining this behavior to YOU? Rate the importance of sustaining this behavior on the 0-10 scale.

Now, look at the benefits side. On that scale of 0-10, how important is the desired result to YOU?

Compare the two results. What do you notice? What can you do to tip the balance in favor of successful goal achievement?

End Self-Sabotage

Self-sabotage is behavior that interferes with achievement of goals. Self-sabotage includes a range of behaviors including negative self-talk ("I can't do this), procrastination (I will start tomorrow), as well as the use of alcohol, drugs, smoking, and comfort eating (I need this to feel better in the moment). It's the reason many people do not achieve their goals.

Meet The "Big Players" In Self-Sabotage

Self-sabotage can stem from many areas within. Some of what I call the "big players" are a lack of self-confidence, lack of self-worth, feelings of unworthiness, a need for control, and the urge to revert back to what we consider comfortable, easy, or familiar.

To take control of self-sabotaging behaviors, it is important that we search deep into our inner selves and become more self-aware. We must identify these behaviors in order to address them.

When one lacks self-confidence, deep down they believe they are unable to achieve success. That belief then dictates the behaviors they choose. They may even have evidence to support this belief. Perhaps they have attempted weight loss multiple times without success. Perhaps they have attempted gambling or smoking cessation multiple times without meeting success. Perhaps they have been programmed to believe they aren't capable of succeeding.

When one lacks self-worth, deep down they believe they are unworthy of achieving success. They may believe they don't deserve to be successful or to live a happier life. They may even feel guilty for being successful.

Perhaps you are in fear of failure once again. If you set yourself up for failure with self-sabotaging behaviors, you know what the outcome will be. Knowing what the outcome will be gives a person a sense of control over the situation.

There are no unknowns, only knowns. Who am I talking to? Keep in mind that although some people welcome and embrace change, for many, change is uncomfortable.

Why They Work Against Us

Self-sabotaging behaviors are there to keep us in our comfort zone. The brain believes that the comfort zone is the safest place for you, and since it is tasked with your survival, safety comes first!

Keep in mind that although some people welcome and embrace change, for many, change is uncomfortable. It is human nature to seek comfort. When we begin to feel a sense of discomfort, we have the tendency to revert back to what is familiar, easy, and comfortable. You know, life as we know it. Again, be aware of this feeling, acknowledge it, validate it, and let it go.

Be mindful that you are creating a new comfortable place, and that will take some time. Remember the chapter on neural pathways. Creating change will take approximately 28 days. The side effect of discomfort will disappear, I promise, as your brain begins to adjust to the new normal, you will be internally rewarded with feelings of happiness, success, and inner peace.

Changing The Way We Think

Lies such as "I'm not worthy" or "I'm doomed to fail" or "I need this to comfort me" must be erased and replaced. Daily positive affirmations will give you the ability to change the way you think.

Each and every one of us possesses the ability to change our thoughts. This power lies within our own self. No other person is able to control our thoughts unless we allow them. Do not surrender your power to anything or anyone external.

Imagine yourself surrounded by a protective bubble, and do not allow the thoughts and ideas others have for you, or about you, to penetrate that bubble. It is time, right here and right now, to make the decision to get out of your own way! Following the RONs will absolutely give you the tools necessary to make this happen.

Listen to what I describe as "Erasing the Habit or Thought." Erasing a habit or negative thought is a concept I have personally used with success. When you are about to act without intention, or speak negatively about yourself, visualize yourself erasing the thought or behavior from a dry erase board. Next, visualize yourself writing the desired thought or behavior on the same board. Use this technique to erase negative self-talk, replacing that internal chatter with positive affirmations.

Develop Your Action Plan

An action plan is an essential tool to carry in your toolbox while embarking on the path of change. I believe I hear you thinking to yourself, "What the #$%@ is an action plan?" Relax my friend, not only am I going to tell you, I am going to teach you how to create your very own action plan!

The Nine Part Plan

An action plan is your very own rulebook for a course of action for change. It is designed to keep you on track and moving forward towards your goals. It includes a plan for overcoming potential barriers that may arise while attempting to implement your chosen course of action. The Action Plan involves several steps that must be taken in order to remain focused and "on track." An action plan has, you guessed it, NINE components!

Here are the NINE steps to "kick" your habits and create new, healthier habits for a new healthier YOU!

1. Identify the habit you would like to change. (The "whats")
2. Identify the importance of this habit change. (The "whys" on a 0-10 scale)
3. Set new habits or "Goals for Change." (The "hows")
4. Visualize how your life will improve once you "kick the habit." (The "payoff")
5. "Declutter" your physical and mental space.
6. Identify potential "barriers" and develop a strategy for overcoming those barriers. (Meditation)
7. Formulate a "plan of action" as to how you will carry out these goals. (Action Plan)
8. Perform your new habits (behaviors) for 28 days. (INTENTION)
9. Celebrate your success! (Achievement)

Recommended: Use The Included Journal

For your benefit, the journal associated with this book, "The Rule of Nines Journal for Success" is included in the back of this book. It is highly recommended that you use it to help keep you focused while creating self-awareness. You can do all of the exercises in it. At the end of your first 28 days, you can purchase the journal separately as you adjust your action plan based on the results from your first 28-day journey.

Tips For Success

- Follow the RONs.
- Keep the "Rule of Nines Journal For Success."
- Write down your RONs: Your "whats", "whys", "hows," and "payoffs"
- Mark a target date on your calendar for both micro and macro goals.
- Nine minutes in the morning and nine minutes in the evening: Read your RONs each morning and write your plan for the day in your journal. Read your RONs each night just before bed and write about your successes in your journal.
- Keeping track: It is important that you keep a calendar or planner. In the calendar, write your deadlines for your goals. Make sure you schedule time in your calendar to journal each morning and night. It is also important you schedule time in your calendar to take action each day towards goal achievement. If you do not take control of your YOU time, it can become challenging to "find time" to fit ourselves in.
- Act with Intention: Wait 5 seconds before acting.
- Don't talk yourself out of acting: Act within 5 seconds.

DAILY AFFIRMATION:

"Addiction is a lie we have been taught to believe. Addictions are merely habits, and habits can be changed."

Kathlyn Heim

FINAL THOUGHTS

N ow that you have the necessary tools for success in your toolbox, it is time to take action! No one can do this for you. Change is a choice.

You owe it to yourself to live your best possible life. As my mentor once told me, "Don't die with the light still burning inside you."

Nameste,

K A T H L Y N

Heim

THE RULE OF NINES

Daily Journal For Success
Meditation, Affirmation, Gratitude

A DAILY JOURNAL
FOR SUCCESS

It is my experience that the combination of daily journaling and meditation greatly increase one's ability to remain focused. As you read and re-write your affirmations and goals daily, the words you write will become your thoughts, your words, your actions, and your destiny.

I commit myself to living my best life possible.

Name

_____

Date

_____

Meditation

Meditation is a habitual process of training your mind to focus and redirect your thoughts. Meditation has been scientifically proven to reduce stress and anxiety, decrease depression and increase positive mood and outlook, improve physical and emotional health, enhance self-awareness, control pain, improve sleep, and help change habits and fight addictions.

The great thing about meditation is that it can be done just about anywhere. When applying the Rule of Nines (RONs) it is important to schedule nine minutes each morning upon awaking, and 9 minutes each evening just before sleep.

If you are a 'newbie" at meditation, do not worry! Just follow the steps below. You will progress from novice to expert in no time at all!

Step One: Sit or lie comfortably.

Step Two: Close your eyes.

Step Three: Inhale deeply. Breathe through the nose while counting to five, then exhale through the mouth counting to five. Repeat this three times.

Step Four: Breathe normally. Focus your attention on your breath and how the body feels and moves with each inhalation and exhalation. If your mind begins to wander, briefly acknowledge the thought, let it go, and refocus on your breathing.

Positive Affirmations

Write at least one down each morning just prior to meditation. Read it again each night.

What is an affirmation? Affirmations are thoughts and statements that we repeat over and over in our mind. In general, these affirmations are coming from our subconscious mind, meaning we are not aware of them. Affirmations are the constant "chatter" going on in our heads. Sometimes these affirmations are negative and self-destructive or self-limiting and are a barrier to our success.

The good news is that through daily positive affirmations, we can re-program our subconscious mind to replace these negative affirmations with positive affirmations. How do we do this? We write down at least one positive self-affirmation daily just prior to our nine-minute meditation.

What is the "payoff" of all this? Writing and speaking positive affirmations daily will retrain your thoughts, your words, your actions, and therefore your destiny. Sound familiar? Remember the chapter in the book about neural pathways or brain pathways? Affirmations are another way we can re-train our brain and create new thoughts and habits.

Gratitude

Gratitude is the expression of thankfulness and gratefulness. It is the feeling of appreciation. Write 3 things you are grateful for each evening and read them aloud each morning.

"Today I am going to love myself with all my heart"

- Kathlyn Heim

Week One

DAY ONE

AM:

Affirmation (write)

_____

9-minute meditation

_____

Goals (write)

_____

Daily Plan:

_____

_____

PM:

Affirmation (read)

_____

9-minute meditation

_____

Gratitude (write)

_____

Goals (write)

_____

_____

_____

_____

_____

_____

_____

_____

_____

_____

_____

_____

_____

_____

_____

_____

_____

_____

DAY TWO

AM:

Affirmation (write)

_____

9-minute meditation

_____

Goals (write)

_____

Daily Plan:

_____

_____

PM:

Affirmation (read)

_____

9-minute meditation

_____

Gratitude (write)

_____

Goals (write)

_____

_____

DAY THREE

AM:

Affirmation (write)

_____

9-minute meditation

_____

Goals (write)

_____

Daily Plan:

_____

_____

PM:

Affirmation (read)

_____

9-minute meditation

_____

Gratitude (write)

_____

Goals (write)

_____

_____

DAY FOUR

AM:

Affirmation (write)

_____

9-minute meditation

_____

Goals (write)

_____

Daily Plan:

_____

_____

PM:

Affirmation (read)

_____

9-minute meditation

_____

Gratitude (write)

_____

Goals (write)

_____

_____

DAY FIVE

AM:

Affirmation (write)

9-minute meditation

Goals (write)

Daily Plan:

PM:

Affirmation (read)

9-minute meditation

Gratitude (write)

Goals (write)

DAY SIX

AM:

Affirmation (write)

_____

9-minute meditation

_____

Goals (write)

_____

Daily Plan:

_____

_____

PM:

Affirmation (read)

_____

9-minute meditation

_____

Gratitude (write)

_____

Goals (write)

_____

_____

DAY SEVEN

AM:

Affirmation (write)

_____

9-minute meditation

_____

Goals (write)

_____

Daily Plan:

_____

_____

PM:

Affirmation (read)

_____

9-minute meditation

_____

Gratitude (write)

_____

Goals (write)

_____

_____

_____

_____

_____

_____

_____

_____

_____

_____

_____

_____

_____

_____

_____

_____

_____

_____

_____

"*Each sunrise brings with it light and hope for new beginnings.*"

– *Kathlyn Heim*

Week Two

DAY ONE

AM:

Affirmation (write)

_____

9-minute meditation

_____

Goals (write)

_____

Daily Plan:

_____

_____

PM:

Affirmation (read)

_____

9-minute meditation

_____

Gratitude (write)

_____

Goals (write)

_____

_____

DAY TWO

AM:

Affirmation (write)

_____

9-minute meditation

_____

Goals (write)

_____

Daily Plan:

_____

_____

PM:

Affirmation (read)

_____

9-minute meditation

_____

Gratitude (write)

_____

Goals (write)

_____

_____

DAY THREE

AM:

Affirmation (write)

_____

9-minute meditation

_____

Goals (write)

_____

Daily Plan:

_____

_____

PM:

Affirmation (read)

_____

9-minute meditation

_____

Gratitude (write)

_____

Goals (write)

_____

_____

DAY FOUR

AM:

Affirmation (write)

_____

9-minute meditation

_____

Goals (write)

_____

Daily Plan:

_____

_____

PM:

Affirmation (read)

_____

9-minute meditation

_____

Gratitude (write)

_____

Goals (write)

_____

_____

DAY FIVE

AM:
Affirmation (write)

_____

9-minute meditation

_____

Goals (write)

_____

Daily Plan:

_____

_____

PM:
Affirmation (read)

_____

9-minute meditation

_____

Gratitude (write)

_____

Goals (write)

_____

_____

_____

_____

_____

_____

_____

_____

_____

_____

_____

_____

_____

_____

_____

_____

_____

_____

_____

DAY SIX

AM:

Affirmation (write)

_____

9-minute meditation

_____

Goals (write)

_____

Daily Plan:

_____

_____

PM:

Affirmation (read)

_____

9-minute meditation

_____

Gratitude (write)

_____

Goals (write)

_____

_____

_____

_____

_____

_____

_____

_____

_____

_____

_____

_____

_____

_____

_____

_____

_____

_____

_____

DAY SEVEN

AM:
Affirmation (write)

_____

9-minute meditation

_____

Goals (write)

_____

Daily Plan:

_____

_____

PM:
Affirmation (read)

_____

9-minute meditation

_____

Gratitude (write)

_____

Goals (write)

_____

_____

"*The best way to achieve success tomorrow is to prepare today.*"

– Kathlyn Heim

Week Three

DAY ONE

AM:

Affirmation (write)

9-minute meditation

Goals (write)

Daily Plan:

PM:

Affirmation (read)

9-minute meditation

Gratitude (write)

Goals (write)

DAY TWO

AM:

Affirmation (write)

_____

9-minute meditation

_____

Goals (write)

_____

Daily Plan:

_____

_____

PM:

Affirmation (read)

_____

9-minute meditation

_____

Gratitude (write)

_____

Goals (write)

_____

_____

DAY THREE

AM:

Affirmation (write)

_____

9-minute meditation

_____

Goals (write)

_____

Daily Plan:

_____

_____

PM:

Affirmation (read)

_____

9-minute meditation

_____

Gratitude (write)

_____

Goals (write)

_____

_____

DAY FOUR

AM:

Affirmation (write)

_____

9-minute meditation

_____

Goals (write)

_____

Daily Plan:

_____

_____

PM:

Affirmation (read)

_____

9-minute meditation

_____

Gratitude (write)

_____

Goals (write)

_____

_____

DAY FIVE

AM:

Affirmation (write)

_____

9-minute meditation

_____

Goals (write)

_____

Daily Plan:

_____

_____

PM:

Affirmation (read)

_____

9-minute meditation

_____

Gratitude (write)

_____

Goals (write)

_____

_____

DAY SIX

AM:

Affirmation (write)

_____

9-minute meditation

_____

Goals (write)

_____

Daily Plan:

_____

_____

PM:

Affirmation (read)

_____

9-minute meditation

_____

Gratitude (write)

_____

Goals (write)

_____

_____

_____

_____

_____

_____

_____

_____

_____

_____

_____

_____

_____

_____

_____

_____

_____

_____

_____

_____

DAY SEVEN

AM:

Affirmation (write)

_____

9-minute meditation

_____

Goals (write)

_____

Daily Plan:

_____

_____

PM:

Affirmation (read)

_____

9-minute meditation

_____

Gratitude (write)

_____

Goals (write)

_____

_____

_____

_____

_____

_____

_____

_____

_____

_____

_____

_____

_____

_____

_____

_____

_____

_____

_____

"Do not let the world tell you who you are."

– Kathlyn Heim

Week Four

DAY ONE

AM:

Affirmation (write)

_____

9-minute meditation

_____

Goals (write)

_____

Daily Plan:

_____

_____

PM:

Affirmation (read)

_____

9-minute meditation

_____

Gratitude (write)

_____

Goals (write)

_____

_____

_____

_____

_____

_____

_____

_____

_____

_____

_____

_____

_____

_____

_____

_____

_____

_____

_____

DAY TWO

AM:

Affirmation (write)

_____

9-minute meditation

_____

Goals (write)

_____

Daily Plan:

_____

_____

PM:

Affirmation (read)

_____

9-minute meditation

_____

Gratitude (write)

_____

Goals (write)

_____

_____

DAY THREE

AM:

Affirmation (write)

_____

9-minute meditation

_____

Goals (write)

_____

Daily Plan:

_____

_____

PM:

Affirmation (read)

_____

9-minute meditation

_____

Gratitude (write)

_____

Goals (write)

_____

_____

DAY FOUR

AM:

Affirmation (write)

_____

9-minute meditation

_____

Goals (write)

_____

Daily Plan:

_____

_____

PM:

Affirmation (read)

_____

9-minute meditation

_____

Gratitude (write)

_____

Goals (write)

_____

_____

DAY FIVE

AM:

Affirmation (write)

_____

9-minute meditation

_____

Goals (write)

_____

Daily Plan:

_____

_____

PM:

Affirmation (read)

_____

9-minute meditation

_____

Gratitude (write)

_____

Goals (write)

_____

_____

DAY SIX

AM:

Affirmation (write)

_____

9-minute meditation

_____

Goals (write)

_____

Daily Plan:

_____

_____

PM:

Affirmation (read)

_____

9-minute meditation

_____

Gratitude (write)

_____

Goals (write)

_____

_____

_____

_____

_____

_____

_____

_____

_____

_____

_____

_____

_____

_____

_____

_____

_____

_____

_____

DAY SEVEN

AM:

Affirmation (write)

_____

9-minute meditation

_____

Goals (write)

_____

Daily Plan:

_____

_____

PM:

Affirmation (read)

_____

9-minute meditation

_____

Gratitude (write)

_____

Goals (write)

_____

_____

Congratulations!

You have completed your first 28 days on your road to behavioral change. It's time to re-evaluate your "Whats" and your "Hows." What is working for you? Are there any changes to be made? How do you feel?

ABOUT THE AUTHOR

Health and wellness coach, Kathlyn Heim, created the Rule of Nines, her method for building the life you have dreamed about but have yet to achieve. Her inspiration came from her personal experiences with both failure and success.

Kathlyn was raised in the San Fernando Valley area of Los Angeles, California. She spent a lot of her childhood reading, going to the library, and wrote a book at age ten. She spent the first ten years of her career working as a Los Angeles Police Officer and Detective, including two years of undercover work in the Prostitution Enforcement Detail of LAPD's Hollywood Division before becoming a registered nurse. Kathlyn's background in Emergency Nursing, Care Management, and Clinical Education has provided her the opportunity to develop training and educational curriculum for Nurse Care Managers for several major healthcare companies.

As a Clinical Educator, Kathlyn educates nurses and patients on how to evoke change from within, improve their health, achieve wellness, and live longer, healthier, happier live. Her personal struggles with eliminating undesirable habits, making lifestyle changes, as well as the burning desire to help others identify goals and overcome life challenges, inspired her to write her book, The Rule of Nines: Live Less Out of Habit, More Out of Intention.

Her book, and associated journal, provides tools along with a simple and unique approach to goal identification, achievement, and personal success. Kathlyn believes that each individual has inherent worth and value, as well as the internal strength and ability to make lifestyle and behavioral changes, thus achieving success in creating and living the life they dream about. Connect with Kathlyn to begin your journey!

Heim supports local communities, raise awareness and funds for single mothers facing catastrophic life challenges. A percentage of all book sales goes towards the fund.

Connect With Kathlyn Online:

Facebook: https://www.facebook.com/The-Rule-of-Nines-334943953757114/
Twitter: https://twitter.com/HeimKathlyn
Instagram: https://www.instagram.com/ruleofnines/
YouTube: https://www.youtube.com/channel/UCXyhD-W8IsZuIVr5isEL4cvg
Website: www.LoveYouLiveYou.com
Email: kathlyn@loveyouliveyou.com

FREE OFFER

Visit my website, www.LoveYouLiveYou.com, and sign up to receive a FREE 8 ½ x 11" poster of The Rule of Nines. It will help you remember the rules so you can stay focused on your goals as you work toward your dreams. Post it in your office at work or affix it to your refrigerator. Keep the Rule of Nines in mind!

Readers Loved, Reviewers Adored

Please help me make this book the best it can be and consider leaving an honest review of the content wherever you purchased this book. Also, if you want to stay up-to-date on the latest news and opportunities to get more help with your goals and dreams, like my Facebook Fan Page.

CPSIA information can be obtained
at www.ICGtesting.com
Printed in the USA
LVHW090104211219
641326LV00001B/130/P